History's Most Murderous Villains

Attila the Hun

Enemy of Ancient Rome

By Arthur K. Britton

Gareth Stevens Publishing

Please visit our website, www.garethstevens.com. For a free color catalog of all our high-quality books, call toll free 1-800-542-2595 or fax 1-877-542-2596.

Library of Congress Cataloging-in-Publication Data

Names: Britton, Arthur K., author.
Title: Attila the Hun / Arthur K. Britton.
Description: New York : Gareth Stevens Publishing, [2016] | Series: History's most murderous villains | Includes index.
Identifiers: LCCN 2015047565 | ISBN 9781482447804 (pbk.) | ISBN 9781482447828 (library bound) | ISBN 9781482447811 (6 pack)
Subjects: LCSH: Attila, -453–Juvenile literature. | Huns–Biography–Juvenile literature. | Huns–History–Juvenile literature.
Classification: LCC D141 .B75 2016 | DDC 936/.03092–dc23
LC record available at http://lccn.loc.gov/2015047565

First Edition

Published in 2017 by
Gareth Stevens Publishing
111 East 14th Street, Suite 349
New York, NY 10003

Designer: Katelyn E. Reynolds
Editor: Therese Shea

Photo credits: Cover, p. 1 (Attila) Hulton Archive/Getty Images; cover, pp. 1–32 (background texture) Eky Studio/Shutterstock.com; cover, pp. 1–32 (blood background) Kjpargeter/Shutterstock.com; cover, pp. 1–32 (grunge banner) Miloje/Shutterstock.com; p. 5 Chris 73/Wikipedia.org; p. 7 ullstein bild/Getty Images; p. 8 orin/Shutterstock.com; p. 9 samxmeg/E+/Getty Images; pp. 11, 12 Time Life Pictures/Mansell/The LIFE Picture Collection/Getty Images; p. 15 Leemage/Universal Images Group/Getty Images; p. 17 (bust) DEA/G. DAGLI ORTI/De Agostini/Getty Images; p. 17 (coin) DeAgostini/Getty Images; p. 19 Fulvio314/Wikipedia.org; p. 21 (icons) MapMaster/Wikipedia.org; p. 21 (map) Alexrk2/Wikipedia.org; p. 22 Apic/Getty Images; p. 25 Independent Picture Service/UIG via Getty Images; p. 26 Wandalstouring/Wikipedia.org; p. 29 Prisma/UIG via Getty Images.

Printed in the United States of America

CPSIA compliance information: Batch #CS16GS: For further information contact Gareth Stevens, New York, New York at 1-800-542-2595.

CONTENTS

Words in the glossary appear in **bold** type the first time they are used in the text.

THE "SCOURGE OF GOD"

The ancient Romans called him the "**Scourge** of God." He liked the nickname so much he adopted it. That name has echoed through history, causing fear and trembling, as has his true name—Attila, king of the Huns.

We know surprisingly little about Attila. We know he died in AD 453. But we don't know when he was born or what his birth name was. "Attila" means "Little Father" and was probably the name he received upon becoming king. As a young man, he learned archery, sword fighting, and how to ride and care for horses. He even learned siege warfare, likely from Roman prisoners.

We also know surprisingly little about the Huns. And to understand Attila, we must first understand something about the Huns.

TERRIBLE TRUTHS

Attila's father's name was Mundzuk, but his mother's name is unknown. He had an older brother, Bleda.

An Ancient Account of Attila

The historian Jordanes, writing about a century after Attila died, had this to say: "He was a man born into the world to shake the nations, the scourge of all lands, who in some way terrified all mankind by the rumors noised abroad concerning him. He was haughty [lordly] in his walk . . . so that the power of his proud spirit appeared in the movement of his body. He was indeed a lover of war."

No portraits of Attila from his lifetime exist. All we have are images created by later artists showing what they imagined Attila might have looked like.

BARBARIANS FROM NOWHERE

The ancient Romans saw the Huns as savage and beastly—in a word, as barbarians. The word "barbarian" comes from the Greek word *barbaros*, which means "foreign, rude, brutal [harsh]." The Huns weren't the only people the Romans considered barbarians, but they were seen as the worst.

In spite of the Romans' critical view of Hun society, they felt a grudging admiration for the Huns' fighting abilities. The Huns were renowned especially for their skill with bow and arrows. One Roman historian wrote: "It must be owned that they are the most terrible of warriors because they fight at a distance with missile weapons having sharpened bones admirably fastened to the shaft. When in close combat with swords, they fight without regard to their own safety."

Terrible Truths

The ancient writer Jordanes thought Huns were the children of witches and demons, or evil spirits.

The Worst of the Worst

Around AD 395, Roman historian Ammianus Marcellinus wrote this about the Huns: "The nation of the Huns surpasses all other barbarians in wildness of life. And though [the Huns] do just bear the likeness of men (of a very ugly pattern), they are so little advanced in civilization that they make no use of fire . . . in the preparation of their food, but feed upon the roots which they find in the fields, and the half-raw flesh of any sort of animal."

The Huns' wildness in battle is reflected in the frightening faces of these charging warriors.

"Scarcely Human"

Jordanes had many unkind things to say about the Huns. He wrote that they were a "savage race, which dwelt at first in the swamps, a **stunted**, foul and puny tribe, scarcely human and having no language save one which bore but slight resemblance to human speech." He went on to note "they were fond of hunting and had no skill in any other art."

Is Kazakhstan the original home of the Huns?

The ancient Romans knew nothing about the Huns' origin except that they came from the East. Roman historian Ammianus Marcellinus didn't even try to guess where. The ancient writer Jordanes had a theory. He guessed their home was the swamp on the eastern shore of the Sea of Azov, which lies just north of the Black Sea.

Modern scholars are equally uncertain about the Huns' origin. For centuries, some scholars thought they might have been the mysterious Xiongnu people. These people attacked China from the north between about 200 BC and AD 200. Recent discoveries indicate it's unlikely the two groups were the same. Many scholars now think the Huns probably came from the area that's today Kazakhstan.

Terrible Truths

The Huns were a **nomadic** people who raised livestock. Those words create a portrait that sounds harmless because they omit such facts as the Huns' military skill and conquests.

THE HORRID HUNNIC EMPIRE

In AD 91, the historian Tacitus became the first Roman to mention the Huns. At that time, the Huns were living around the Caspian Sea and didn't seem to present any unusual threat. When Roman historian Ammianus Marcellinus wrote about the Huns 300 years later, he reported they didn't have settled homes or kings. Instead, each nomadic group had its own leader. Yet by that time, the Huns had overrun the modern countries of Hungary and Romania and forced the barbarian peoples occupying those regions to flee into Roman territory.

The Huns were building an empire. It wasn't like the Roman Empire, with a single ruler and a central governing city. But it was an empire in the sense of being a vast territory controlled by the Huns.

Terrible Truths

As the Huns conquered new territory, they struck without warning and didn't hesitate to kill women and children as well as enemy soldiers.

Swift and Sudden

Ammianus Marcellinus wrote this about the Huns' fierce and uncommon fighting methods: "[T]hey fight in no regular order of battle, but by being extremely swift and sudden in their movements, they disperse [scatter], and then rapidly come together again in loose array, spread havoc [confusion] over vast plains, and flying over the **rampart**, they **pillage** the camp of their enemy almost before he has become aware of their approach."

According to ancient reports, the Huns' horses would actually join in the fighting during battles, using their teeth and hoofs.

The Hun Warrior

Hun fighters wore layers of heavy leather that had been heavily coated with animal fat. This made the leather soft and bendable and able to resist rain. Leather-covered, steel-lined helmets protected their head. **Chain mail** around their neck and shoulders supplied further protection against arrows and swords. They wore soft leather boots that were excellent for riding, although they were useless for marching or fighting on foot.

French painter Georges-Antoine Rochegrosse imagines the Huns pillaging a Roman household in this work from 1910.

The Huns finally entered Roman territories in AD 395, destroying cities and farmland in Thrace and Syria. However, Huns were also serving in the Roman army and settled in other Roman territories. This may seem odd, but remember, the Huns weren't united under a single leader. Each group had its own leader and followed its own course.

In AD 408, a group of Huns under the leadership of Uldin pillaged Thrace. The Romans couldn't fight them off, so they offered Uldin gold instead. He wanted too much, so they paid his officers to stop the pillaging. This worked, and from then on, the Romans kept the peace by paying the Huns.

The Huns also acquired gold through plunder and by selling their prisoners back to Rome. They soon obtained great wealth.

Terrible Truths

According to Ammianus Marcellinus, when the Huns appeared, it seemed to the Romans "that a race of men, hitherto unknown, had suddenly descended like a whirlwind from the lofty mountains, as if they had risen from some secret recess of the earth, and were ravaging and destroying everything which came in their way."

A Murderous Villain's Childhood

Besides not knowing when Attila was born or what his birth name was, we don't know where he was born. We don't know what language Attila and the Huns spoke. So what do we know?

We know the Romans knew his uncle, Rugila (or Rua), as king of the Huns. We're not sure if that means all Huns were united under Rugila or if he simply ruled the largest group. In any event, it means Attila and his brother, Bleda, were members of a royal family and thus had privileged childhoods. In preparation for leadership, they're believed to have been present at war councils and **negotiations** starting at a young age. And when Rugila died around AD 434, the brothers took control and ruled jointly.

Terrible Truths

Some scholars think Rugila may have had sons who would have come to power after him, but Attila and Bleda killed them so they could rule instead.

What Did Attila Look Like?

We can only imagine what Attila looked like. Nomadic peoples don't make portraits. The historian Jordanes left an account, which was written about a century after Attila died, but based on one written during his lifetime: "He was short of stature, with a broad chest and a large head; his eyes were small, his beard was thin and sprinkled with gray. He had a flat nose and a swarthy [dark] **complexion**."

This portrait of Attila, produced more than 1,000 years after he died, shows him with dark skin and a flat nose. It also shows him with goatlike horns, to suggest a beastly and demonic nature.

THE REIGN OF THE DREADFUL DUO

When Attila and Bleda came to power in AD 434, the Roman Empire was divided into two parts. The Western Roman Empire had its capital in Rome, and the Eastern Roman Empire had its capital in Constantinople (modern Istanbul, Turkey).

The brothers made a treaty with the Eastern Empire that, among other things, required the empire to pay them 700 pounds (318 kg) of gold each year. The brothers claimed the empire didn't fulfill the treaty requirements. Attila attacked and destroyed the empire's army. A new treaty was made, and the empire then had to pay 2,100 pounds (953 kg) of gold each year!

Over 10 years, the Huns invaded lands that are today Hungary, Greece, Spain, and Italy. They burned towns and killed the people living there.

TERRIBLE TRUTHS

The Huns under Attila and Bleda captured lots of riches, but some scholars think the Huns weren't in it just for wealth. They think the Huns truly enjoyed warfare.

Homeless and Lawless

Once again, Ammianus Marcellinus supplies information about the Huns: "None of them plow, or even touch a plow handle, for they have no settled abode, but are homeless and lawless, perpetually wandering with their wagons, which they make their homes . . . This active and indomitable [unconquerable] race, being excited by an unrestrained desire of plundering the possessions of others, went on ravaging and slaughtering all the nations in their neighborhood."

‹ Theodosius II

Valentinian III ›

Theodosius II, the emperor of the Eastern Empire, and Valentinian III, the emperor of the Western Empire, both gave gold to Attila and Bleda to keep the peace.

ATTILA BECOMES KING

In AD 445, Attila became the sole king of the Huns. Bleda disappeared from historical records—no further mention of him appears anywhere. What happened to him? Some sources seem to indicate Bleda was killed fighting. However, according to the Roman historian Priscus, "Bleda, king of the Huns, was assassinated [murdered] as a result of the plots of his brother Attila." Since Priscus is considered the most reliable source about the Huns, most scholars believe Attila had his brother murdered.

Once he became the sole king, Attila ruled as an autocrat. That is, he ruled with unlimited authority. In AD 447, he once again attacked the Eastern Empire. The negotiations that followed took 3 years, and the treaty that resulted was, of course, in Attila's favor.

TERRIBLE TRUTHS

In his attack on the Eastern Empire, Attila destroyed over 70 cities and took survivors as slaves.

Attila the Temperate

Priscus met and dined with Attila in AD 448. He provided this account: "A luxurious meal, served on silver plate, had been made ready for us and the barbarian guests, but Attila ate nothing but meat on a wooden trencher [tray]. In everything else, too, he showed himself temperate—his cup was of wood, while to the guests were given **goblets** of gold and silver. His dress, too, was quite simple, affecting only to be clean."

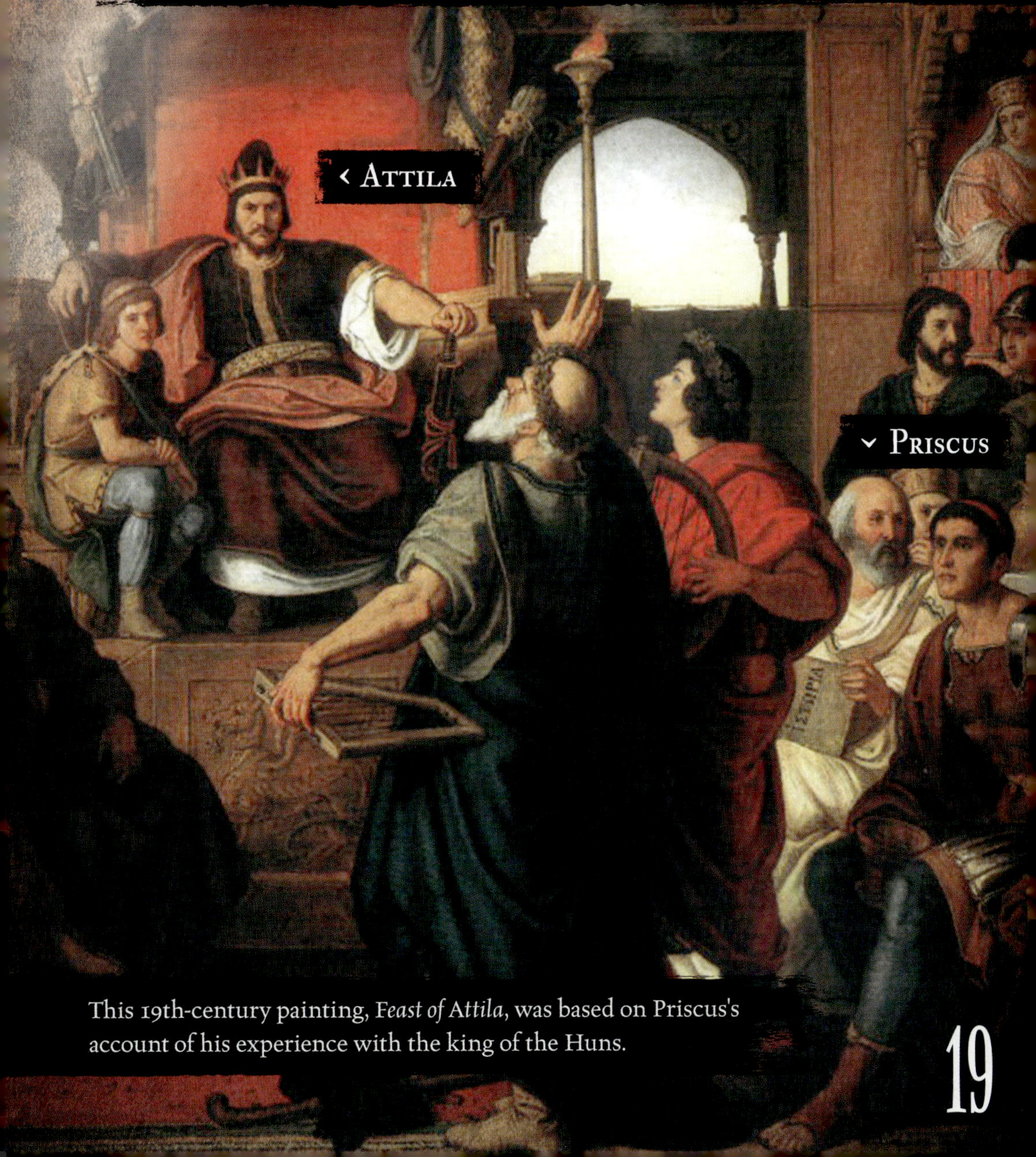

This 19th-century painting, *Feast of Attila*, was based on Priscus's account of his experience with the king of the Huns.

ATTILA'S HUNS
SWARM ACROSS GAUL

Attila turned his attention to the Western Empire. In AD 451, he launched an invasion of Gaul, which was the name used for the territory that now makes up France and Belgium. He set out with about 200,000 to 500,000 warriors.

The Huns took modern-day Belgium easily. They encountered no resistance when they reached the towns of Trier and Metz, and they slaughtered the citizens. The Huns went on from there, destroying everything in their path. At this point, it must have seemed to Attila—and perhaps to the people of Gaul—that this would end the way Attila's campaigns always ended. The Huns would triumph, and the Western Empire would have to pay more gold to keep the peace. But that's not what happened.

Terrible Truths

On this campaign, Attila and the Huns plundered and burned to the ground some of the greatest cities of Europe: Reims, Mainz, Strasbourg, Cologne, and Worms.

The Sword of Mars

Attila claimed to have the sword of Mars, the Roman god of war. According to the ancient historian Jordanes, a shepherd found it: "He dug it up and took it straight to Attila. He rejoiced at this gift and, being ambitious, thought he had been appointed ruler of the whole world, and that through the sword of Mars supremacy in all wars was assured to him."

Follow the destructive path of the Huns on this map. Attila's crushing victories ended in Châlons, marked with an X here.

Supremely Brave

The ancient historian Jordanes wrote about the battle and Attila's behavior in the face of defeat: "[Attila] remained supremely brave even in this **extremity** and had heaped up a funeral **pyre** of horse trappings [coverings], so that if the enemy should attack him he was determined to cast himself into the flames; that none might have the joy of wounding him, and that the lord of so many races might not fall into the hands of his foes."

This picture of the Battle of Châlons made centuries later shows how an artist imagines it might have looked.

Roman general Flavius Aetius—who'd spent years with the Huns as a youth—prepared an alliance, or association, to fight the Huns. Aetius reached an agreement with Theodoric I, king of the Visigoths. The Visigoths were barbarians who occupied southwestern Gaul. Normally enemies of the Romans, they joined with them to fight their common enemy, the Huns.

The Romans, Visigoths, and their allies met the Huns and their allies in a great battle that's known by different names, both based on where it took place. It's known as the Battle of the Catalaunian Plains and the Battle of Châlons. It's been called one of the bloodiest battles in history and included the death of Theodoric I. In the end, however, Attila suffered his first defeat and withdrew from Gaul.

Terrible Truths

The battle was costly in terms of human lives. One ancient author writing about it said there were "truly countless bodies."

A WHIRLWIND OF DEATH HITS ITALY

Attila didn't let his defeat in Gaul stop him permanently. In AD 452, he led the Huns on an invasion of Italy. The Huns plundered city after city and met no resistance. The list is long and includes cities such as Aquileia, Padua, Verona, and Milan.

Flavius Aetius couldn't stop the Huns this time. He didn't have a large enough army. Terrified people fled cities and villages looking for someplace they'd be safe from Attila and his warriors. They escaped to the marshes along the northern coast of Italy facing the Adriatic Sea. It worked. The Huns passed and headed toward the city of Rome. Over time, the Romans built houses on dry land in the marshes. Eventually, this area became the city of Venice.

TERRIBLE TRUTHS

The Huns destroyed Aquileia so completely that nothing was left. No one could even tell where it had been.

The Plundering of Aquileia

The historian Jordanes provided the following account of the Huns at Aquileia: "[Attila] rekindled the troops' desire to sack Aquileia. War machines were built, all sorts of engines brought near. Without delay, they entered the city, ransacked [plundered], divided and so cruelly vanquished [defeated] it that scarcely any trace remained to be seen. Then, bolder and not yet satiated [stuffed] with Roman blood, the Huns raged . . . through the remaining Venetian cities."

Experts in archaeology have uncovered remains of some of the buildings the Huns destroyed at Aquileia.

Don't Go to Rome!

According to Jordanes, "When [Attila's] mind turned to approaching Rome . . . his own men dissuaded [discouraged] him, not out of regard for the city to which they were hostile, but because they remembered the example of Alaric the one-time king of the Visigoths. They felt anxiety for the fortune of their own king because, after Alaric had crushed Rome, he did not survive very long but soon departed from human affairs."

The Huns' empire reached its peak under Attila. It stretched from modern-day Russia down through what's today Hungary and across present-day Germany to France (Gaul).

The Huns' trail of death and destruction came to an end at the Apennines, a mountain chain that runs down the length of Italy. **Famine** and a deadly disease called the plague were raging in Italy at the time. They may have forced the Huns to turn back.

It's also been suggested superstition might have played a part. In AD 410, Alaric I died shortly after leading the Visigoths in sacking Rome. The Huns might have believed his death was caused by sacking the great city and the same could happen to Attila.

In addition, we know Pope Leo I went to meet with Attila to ask for peace. We don't know what happened at the meeting, but afterward, Attila turned back and left Italy.

Terrible Truths

The historian Jordanes wrote of the horror the Huns brought to Italy: "In their rage, they turned against neighboring cities and devastated [destroyed] almost all of Italy."

DEATH AND LEGACY

Attila meant to attack the Eastern Empire in AD 453. The emperor, Marcian, refused to pay the Huns the gold he owed. However, the attack never happened. Attila took a new, young wife, and, after a night of celebrating, a blood vessel burst and he choked to death on his own blood.

According to Priscus, his warriors cut their hair and sliced their cheeks "so that the greatest of all warriors should be mourned not with the tears or the wailing of women but with the blood of men." The Huns killed those who buried Attila and his treasures so his grave would never be discovered.

Attila's three sons inherited the empire, but they fought each other for the greatest share. By AD 469, the empire had fallen apart.

Terrible Truths

Jordanes wrote: "His coffins they reinforced, the first with gold, the second with silver, the third with strong iron, making it known that those elements suit an all-powerful king."

Attila for the Modern Age

Today, many people find qualities to admire in Attila. Wess Roberts wrote a best-selling book titled *Leadership Secrets of Attila the Hun* for business executives. He argued that Attila showed a "win-directed, take-charge" management style. George Steinbrenner, who once owned the New York Yankees baseball team, studied Attila hoping to gain wisdom useful for business. And scholars find Attila valued loyalty, was generous, and was a man of his word. Who knew?

Historian Adrian Goldsworthy notes that while there were many barbarian leaders, Attila is the one whose name is still recognized. He's *the* barbarian of the ancient world.

GLOSSARY

chain mail: bendable armor made of connected metal rings

complexion: the appearance of the skin, especially of the face

extremity: a time of extreme danger or critical need

famine: a period of extreme scarcity of food

goblet: a bowl-shaped cup

negotiation: the act or process of meeting and discussing with someone to arrive at an agreement or compromise about something

nomadic: having to do with people who have no fixed residence but wander from place to place, usually seasonally

pillage: to sack or plunder

pyre: a heap of burnable material used to burn a body as part of a funeral ceremony

rampart: a mound of earth raised as protection around a place

scourge: an instrument of punishment

stunted: dwarfed

For More Information

Books

Fields, Nic. *Attila the Hun: Leadership, Strategy, Conflict.* Oxford, UK: Osprey Publishing, 2015.

Price, Sean Stewart. *Attila the Hun: Leader of the Barbarian Hordes.* New York, NY: Franklin Watts, 2009.

Rice, Earle, Jr. *The Life and Times of Attila the Hun.* Hockessin, DE: Mitchell Lane, 2010.

Websites

Attila the Hun
ancienthistory.about.com/cs/attilathehun/a/attilathehun.htm
Read a brief account of Attila's life and death here.

Battle of Chalons: Attila the Hun Versus Flavius Aetius
www.historynet.com/battle-of-chalons-attila-the-hun-versus-flavius-aetius.htm
Read about the only battle Attila ever lost.

Huns
www.ancient.eu/Huns/
Find out more about the Huns on this website.

INDEX